Pride in the En

The Evolution of Swords

John Wilkinson Latham
& Robert Wilkinson Latham

Pooley Sword Ltd
LONDON - SHEFFIELD

The Evolution of Swords, John Wilkinson Latham & Robert Wilkinson Latham

ISBN: 978-1-84336-151-0

Pooley Sword Ltd
1 Highdown House
Shoreham Airport
West Sussex
BN43 5PB

Tel: 01273 467277
Fax: 01273 462461
Email: enquiries@pooleysword.com
www.pooleysword.com

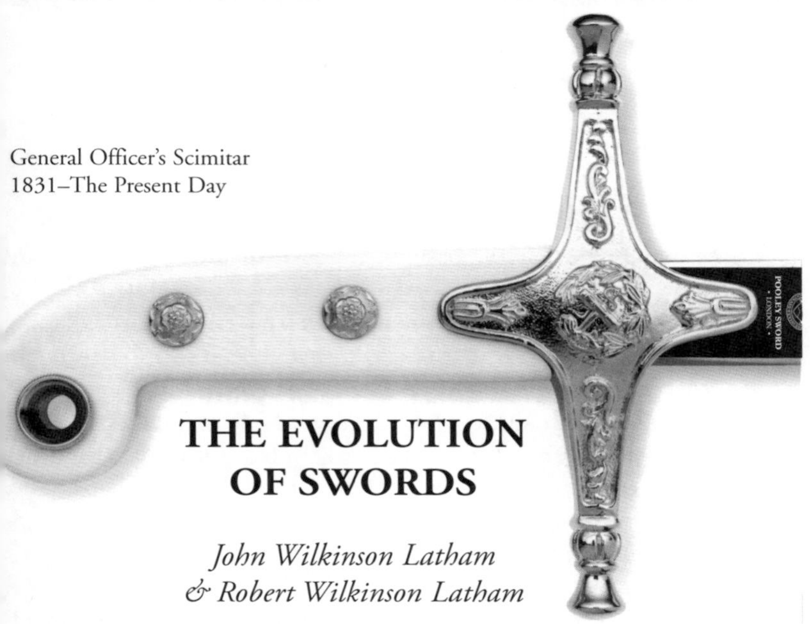

General Officer's Scimitar
1831–The Present Day

THE EVOLUTION OF SWORDS

John Wilkinson Latham
& Robert Wilkinson Latham

The history of swords is nearly as old as the history of man, who found himself naked and unarmed in a world where all his fellow creatures, although inferior in reasoning powers, were armed with horns, antlers, fangs and claws. In order to survive, man had to use his mental powers to outstrip the animals both in attacking and defensive weapons.

Starting with the wooden club and the sharpened stick, both of which survive today in the Drum Major's Mace the Beefeater's Halberd and the lance, the path of development lay through the stone age with its flint axes and arrow heads until the Bronze and Iron Ages, when man first learned to extract copper and tin from ores in the soil and later to extract and purify iron.

The word 'Sword' is derived from the old English word 'Sweord' and it is likely that the Dutch word 'Zwaard' and the German 'Schwert' come from the same stem. The Italian 'Spada' and the Spanish 'Espada' undoubtedly come from the Latin 'Spatha'.

There were two methods of making the first swords from bronze.They were either cast in a mould or hammered out of a lump of bronze, then ground to final shape on stone. The latter method was preferred as it was found that cast bronze was apt to be brittle, whereas forging had the effect of hardening and tempering the metal.

After the sword was made, it was decorated by hand to suit the customer's wishes.

The craft of the swordsmith has changed little since these early days.

True, the blade is now forged from bar steel by mechanical hammers instead of the Smith's mighty arm, and mechanical stamping and acid etching has partially done away with hand decoration, but the craft is about the only one where the basic methods of manufacture date back to the Bronze Age.

The standard service blade commences as a bar of steel 12 inches long by 1 inch wide by ⅝ inch thick. This is heated and drawn out through mechanical hammers to 24 inches by ¾ inch by ¼ inch. It is then reheated and passed through shaped rollers from which it emerges roughly correct in length and shape of the required blade. It is then ground on large stone wheels in the grinding mill to its final correct shape. The blade now passes to the hardening shop where it is hardened, tempered and proved. The final stage is polishing and embossing with the required pattern and insignia.

Manufacture of the hilt depends very much on the type of sword being made. The component parts are either cast in gilding metal or stamped out of brass or steel sheet. These parts are then hand finished and chased before passing to the plating shop where they are fine plated with gold, silver, nickel, rhodium or chromium according to the customer's requirements.

Scabbards are either of steel, leather, wood covered with leather or velvet. Metal scabbards are formed up by hand on steel mandrels from

British Pioneer's Sword
1856–1903

British Heavy Cavalry
Trooper's Sword 1796–1830

sheet steel and after brazing the joints, are ground and polished or plated as required. Wooden scabbard bodies are made by skilled cabinet makers to fit the blade of the individual sword, the leather or velvet covering is then sewn on to this body by hand. Leather scabbards are hand sewn over steel mandrels and then oven baked to harden them.

The variety of pattern in swords is perhaps the main feature which has prevented the craft from dying under pressure of more modern methods. Each and every country has different designs from the others, no two regiments have exactly identical swords, and customers often require special embossing on the blades of their names, ranks etc.

Swords of the Ancient World

The Ancient World is the name given to the World from the dawn of history down until the fall of the Roman Empire, in the 5th Century A.D. The history of the Ancient World is mainly concerned with the rise and fall of the great Empires which existed around the Mediterranean and the valleys of the Nile, Tigris and Euphrates. It also includes India, which in those days was far more civilised than the countries in the Western World.

The oldest of the Empires was probably the Egyptian Empire, united out of lower and upper Egypt by the first king known to history, MENES, in approximately 3400 B.C. This empire existed for nearly three thousand years before falling, first to the Assyrians in 671 B.C., next to the Persians in 525 B.C. and later to Alexander the Great in 332 B.C. On the death of Alexander, after his unsuccessful campaign in India, PTOLEMY became King and his family ruled the land until the Romans under OCTAVIAN routed the armies of Egypt and CLEOPATRA, the vanquished queen, committed suicide by holding an asp to her breast.

The earliest empire in the great plain of the Tigris and Euphrates was the Sumerian, founded by SARGON I about 2750 B.C. Approximately seven centuries later, the Amorites from Syria established themselves in a village, called Babylon, and after conquering neighbouring tribes founded what was to become the great empire of the Babylonians.

The next great empire to arise was that of the Assyrians. They waged constant war against the Hittites from Asia Minor, who are credited with being the first of the ancient peoples to have used iron implements.

The Assyrians conquered Babylon and made war on and defeated the Israelites. In their turn, they were overthrown by the Chaldeans, whose king was NEBUCHADNEZZAR.

The Persians were the next people to rise to power, and under CYRUS THE GREAT they captured Babylon in 539 B.C. Another famous race was the Greeks, who set up a number of city-states until conquered by ALEXANDER THE GREAT.

Rome became the greatest power of them all, under JULIUS CAESAR, whose legions campaigned far and wide, and after a triumphant march across Northern Europe, landed in Britain in 54 B.C. CONSTANTINE (A.D. 306-337), the first Roman Emperor to embrace Christianity, built a new capital on the Bosphorus on the site of the old Greek fortress of Byzantium, and named it Constantinople. The western empire fell in A.D. 476 before the attacks of the Barbarian tribes from the North of Europe. At about this time, Roman Britain was attacked by the Angles and the Saxons, the former leaving the legacy of their name to England (Angleland). Constantinople continued to flourish until at last, in A.D. 1453, it was sacked by the Turks, but fortunately not before the precious relics of Byzantine and Greek Culture were removed to Italy, where they played a big part in the Renaissance, or revival of learning in Europe.

The Egyptian Sword

Documentary evidence of the way of life of the Egyptians is available in abundance, but evidence as to the arms of her soldiers is very scanty. Although there is no doubt that at first they carried bronze swords, none have come down to us intact. A few weapons in iron are exhibited in the museums in London, Paris and, prior to the Second World War, in Berlin.

ASSYRIAN BRONZE SWORD. CIRCA 1300 B.C.

The Assyrian Sword

Almost the entire Assyrian army was armed with the Sword, which was worn on the left side of the body, passed through loops of the belt so that it lay horizontally. The weapon was straight and tapered gradually to a point, its length being about 18 to 22 inches. Most of our knowledge of this weapon comes from monuments and sculptures, on which the sword is seldom shown unsheathed, but we imagine that the blade was two-edged and carried a longitudinal ridge up each side of it.

The hilt was shaped rather like the handle of the modern engineer's file, but was exquisitely worked and decorated. The pommel was most elegant in shape and was invariably enriched with stones and precious metals. The scabbard was usually of hide terminating in a bulbous shape which was always decorated with the figures of reclining lions or other wild animals, their bodies stretched out in the direction of the hilt.

SCANDINAVIAN BRONZE SWORD

The Gallic Sword

The first Gallic sword was of bronze, with a blade of between 18 and 24 inches. It was a two-edged weapon, and the form of the blade has been described as being like a sage leaf, in that it was narrow at the fort and gradually swelled out with a graceful curve to be at its broadest about one third of its length from the point to which it tapered in a convex curve. There were two types of hilt, one being a continuation of the blade from the fort of the same width, pierced with holes, to which pieces of wood or bone could be riveted on each side. The other type was the covering with wood of three bronze rods which were fixed in a large boss at the bottom of the blade, a rather unsatisfactory arrangement.

Their second type of sword, which is thought to have led to their defeat by the Romans, was of iron, a metal which they never managed to attain any skill in working, with the result that their blades were deficient in temper and were apt to bend on striking the shield or cuirass of their opponents. The shape of the blade and the details of the hilt were similar to their bronze weapon.

GREEK BRONZE SWORD

The Greek Sword

The Greek sword of the heroic ages is known to us in some detail from Homer's Illiad.

"Thus as he spoke, his sharp-edged sword he drew, *Ponderous and vast, suspended at his side."*	I1., XXXII, 320.
"Then from beside his thigh Achilles drew his *Trenchant Blade."*	I1., XXI, 192.
"Achilles drew and .... let fall his trenchant sword; *the two-edge blade was buried deep."*	I1., XXXI, 133.
"O'er his shoulders flung his sword, adorned with *silver studs."*	I1., II, 51.
"Around his shoulders slung, his sword he bore, *brass bladed, silver studded."*	I1., III, 390.
"This said, a silver studded sword he gave, *with scabbard and with well-cut belt complete."*	I1., VII, 335.

It is evident from this description that it was a sword for both cutting and thrusting, having a two edged blade made of bronze which we presume tapered to an acute point. The hilt was obviously highly decorated and some authorities state that it had a cross-guard of short, broad quillons whilst others say that there were no quillons and the hilt was a continuation of the blade as in the first type of Gallic hilt quoted above. The scabbard was carried slung on the back, and from Homer's description the sword lay low enough to be against the left thigh. This gives us very little clue as to the length of the blade, but most authorities give it as between 18 and 30 inches.

The Sword of the Historic ages of Greece was at first a copy, in iron, of the sword referred to above. However, there was introduced, very soon a sword which was to be the prototype of the standard Greek Military Sword. It was a much longer weapon, with a straight blade, and it was two-edged. It was therefore still a weapon for both cutting and thrusting. The Greek swordsmiths were very adept at fine ornamentation and they lavished all their skill on the decoration of both the hilt and scabbard of these Swords.

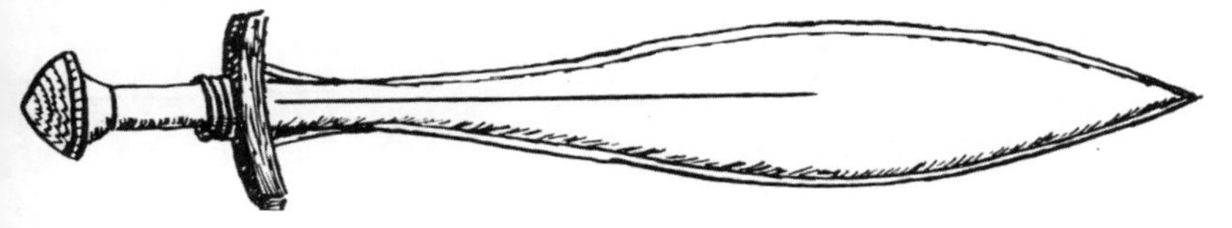

ROMAN IRON SWORD

The Roman Sword

The early Roman Sword, the gladius, was like most bronze swords of that time, a leaf shape, but unlike other nations' weapons the blade was extremely short. There was no cross-guard and the hilt was merely a prolongation of the blade, suitably covered on both sides with either wood or bone.

About the first century B.C. an iron sword was adopted, being two edged with parallel sides and having an obtuse angled point. The hilt had a cross-guard with short quillons having bulbous tips. The grip was either of wood, bone or ivory and swelled out into a globular or shaped pommel, the favourite shape being the head of a wild animal of the species met in the arena.

The sword was carried in an ornamental scabbard, slung on the left side. It is easy to see how the Roman soldiers got their well deserved reputation for bravery, when one considers that to get within killing range with such a short sword, against adversaries armed with the long sword, lance or javelin, must have demanded personal courage of a very high order.

At the end of the 1st Century A.D. we find that the Roman sword is no longer a short weapon and that it has become single-edged. This was the weapon that was called the Spatha and it is shown in use, along with the gladius, in the carvings on the Trajan Column, in Rome.

The Anglo-Saxon Swords

This was essentially a cavalry weapon and was not carried by anyone below the rank of Thane. At first the sword was two-edged and had no cross-guard. The blade swelled out towards the tip and the point was rounded.

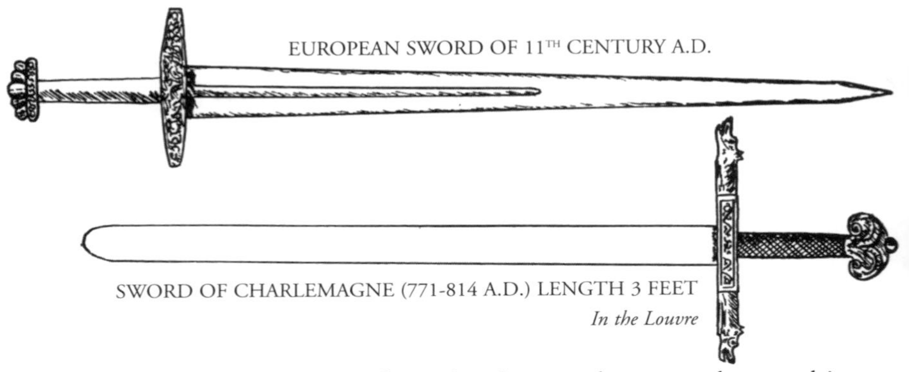

EUROPEAN SWORD OF 11TH CENTURY A.D.

SWORD OF CHARLEMAGNE (771-814 A.D.) LENGTH 3 FEET
In the Louvre

The grip was either of wood or bone and was not decorated in any way. Later the Anglo-Saxon sword became thinner in the blade and acutely pointed. At the same time a cross-guard began to appear and a pommel was used to finish off the grip, both of these parts were now subject to ornamentation.

A sword of this time is preserved in the Wallace Collection at Hertford House, behind Oxford Street, London. The grip is four inches long and the blade is two inches wide at the hilt and thirty inches long.

Swords of the Middle Ages

Possibly the most famous, or should I say infamous, sword that is known to the English speaking nations is that synonym of suspense, the Sword of Damocles. At the beginning of what are called the Middle Ages – about the fifth century A.D. – all the legendary heroes whose names are preserved for us in the many heroic sagas had their Swords, each having a name and each as famous as the wielder himself.

Everyone must have heard of the "Excalibur of King Arthur" and there are many others such as the “Hunting of Beowulf ", "The Alteclre of Olivier", "The Tizona of the Cid", "The Querstenbeis of Haakon" and "The Preciosa of King Poligan" to name just a few. Each one of these was a long iron sword renowned for the temper of the blade and having a hilt which was elaborately chased and then inlaid with precious metals. The owner's name was engraved on the blade in Runic letters, and if we can believe the legends the sword would not be satisfactorily wielded by any other than its owner.

The Franks, a barbarian race which eventually became the conquerors of Rome, were pre-eminent among the warring tribes of Europe for approximately four hundred years from the 5th Century A.D. They were, at first, equipped in the most rudimentary manner with only a shield for defence, an axe or "Francisca", a Lance and a short Sword called a "Scramasax". This weapon was in reality a long Knife and was rarely over 22 inches in length with the blade two inches wide at the hilt, tapering to an acute point. It had a central ridge up both sides of the blade and was hollowed out on each side of this ridge in order that the blade might carry poison.

The true sword of the Franks was carried by the officer or clan chief class. It had a flat, double-edged blade, between thirty and thirty-two inches long and was parallel for most of its length, coming to an obtuse point. It was housed in a scabbard of wood or leather on which was engraved a decorative pattern, which was then filled with copper.

The Frankish sword of the reign of Charlemagne differed very little from the previous pattern, except that the ornamentation of the hilt and cross-guard was far more decorative and the metals used were now the precious kind, such as gold, silver and refined copper. The grip was not solely of wood but more often of ivory or bone and the scabbard was tipped with a chape of metal to prevent wear.

When we are identifying swords of the Middle Ages we are apt to find that historians and sometimes antiquarians base a lot of their descriptive writing on the various tapestries, columns and tombs, which show fighting men of the period concerned, together with their arms and armour. This can be a dangerous practice, as artistic licence has been evoked for as long as artists have practised their art, and the temptation to improve the beauty of a weapon without considering the effect this would have on the balance and utility has in the majority of cases not been resisted. Readers may recall a recent case, in which an equestrian statue in London of a First World War General was found to have its spurs upside down! The swords of the time of the Norman Conquest have been minutely described by some writers by reference to the Bayeux Tapestry, but remembering the warning above, and considering that the tapestry was woven by women who, although artistic, had no technical training and was designed mainly from the descriptions of the returning warriors, it would be dangerous to accept these detailed descriptions. In broad outline, the blade was straight, tapering to an acute point and double-edged. As the Normans were descended from the Saxon and Danish races, this type of blade is to be expected. The quillons are shown on the tapestry to be straight and short, the grip parallel and the pommel spherical. The scabbard was suspended on the left side by a cord around the waist. Later Norman period examples have been discovered with the quillons curving upwards towards the blade.

In case you have been left in suspense by an earlier paragraph, Damocles was one of the courtiers of the elder Dionysius of Syracuse. When he spoke in extravagant terms of the happiness of his sovereign, Dionysius is said to have invited him to a sumptuous banquet at which he found himself seated under a naked sword suspended by a single hair.

From the earliest days up until about the 16th Century, the development of the sword in Europe was very slow and gradual and never really advanced much from the straight, double-edged blade, broad at the hilt and tapering to a point, with a wooden grip, a flat disc-shaped pommel and a straight cross-guard. With this weapon it was possible to thrust, although its main purpose was for cutting, and being a sword of great weight made it unsuitable for guarding, so that the forearm and hand had at first to be covered with a gauntlet of cuir boulli (leather moulded in boiling water) and later by a metal gauntlet.

With the beginning of the 16th Century the firearm began to come into use and with it came the gradual falling into disuse of body armour, which was found to be very little protection against a bullet unless it was thickened up to be of such a weight that a man could hardly carry it.

With the dying out of armour, the science of swordsmanship made very rapid advances, and with these advances came the improvements to the defensive qualities of the sword hilt, to do away with the need for wearing a gauntlet. The ancient type of sword referred to above now developed into the rapier, which had a long, narrow, two-edged blade, very pointed, but still of considerable weight, which was first of all used for both cut and thrust. However, the length soon increased, and with it the blade and hilt were lightened, turning it into a purely thrusting weapon. Soon it became of extravagant length and the hilt became more complicated, with curved guards, counter guards, and very wide cross guards, which protected the hand admirably against the cut, but were not very effectual against the thrust.

Rapiers, of course, were naturally of use for single combat and were, in the main, carried only by Naval and Military officers, the enlisted men being armed with hangers and cutlasses of more simple design but with heavier cutting blades and very little pretence at thrusting qualities.

RIFLE REGIMENT DRUMMER'S SWORD 1857 PATTERN

These alterations to the sword brought in an entirely new science of sword-play which required far greater skill in use. Up to this time swords had been exclusively weapons of war and were not worn with civilian dress, as the poignard and dagger were considered more becoming and more useful if a civilian needed to go armed. From approximately 1525 onwards, the sword was adopted as part of the everyday costume of a gentleman, which brought about an amazing increase in the demand for these weapons and of course a great change in the social customs of the people, mainly owing to the increasing popularity of the unofficial duel and various codes of honour which were imported from the Continent.

The 17th Century brought with it possibly the most popular era of the sword, when the rapier was superseded by a far simpler weapon rather akin to the fencing epee of today. There was, in this century, a great difference of opinion between the Southern and the Northern Europeans as to what constituted the best type of Military sword. The Southerners favoured a light-straight-bladed thrusting weapon, whereas the Northerners began to go in for a heavy, curved cutting weapon. Reference to the build of the people in these parts of Europe shows why this is so, the Mediterranean peoples and the Latins being of light build and very quick on their feet, whereas the Northerners were a heavily built, very strong people but slow and ponderous in their movements.

The Era of Regulation Military Swords

The 18th century heralded the beginning of the equipment of armies to regulation and the documentation of the various patterns of weapons, uniforms and accoutrements. It is probable that the first orders regarding swords came at least a century before, but they were couched in such general terms that they could not be regarded as firm regulations of the exact type or pattern carried.

The forerunners of the regulation armies were without doubt those of Prussia and France and by about 1705, the forces of other European countries had followed suit. The vagueness of these regulations devoid of drawings meant that commanding officers and manufacturers interpreted them widely and in differing ways making the end products as diverse as they had previously been.

In Britain in 1822 many new regulations were promulgated under George IV and in these the descriptions were written in a far less ambiguous way. Actual examples of the swords were lodged at the Tower of London and each was sealed with the mark of the Board of Ordnance. These 'sealed' patterns were made available to the manufacturers who could then see the exact style of the hilt, blade and scabbard. These examples were moved in the mid 19th century to the Royal Small Arms Factory at Enfield and lodged in their famous 'Pattern Room' (Now part of the Royal Armouries in Leeds, UK)

However, the large variety of patterns within individual armies meant that existing styles were copied and adapted by others nations, so there are often marked similarities between say a British sword and one of a certain German State and of course an even closer similarity between British Swords and those carried by the forces of Commonwealth countries.

Most armies had differing patterns for officers, other ranks and special weaponry for Pioneers, musicians, officer cadets, engineers and quasi- military forces such as police. In Germany, even firemen had swords!

The predominant user of the sword in armies of the of the late 18th and 19th centuries was the cavalry, foot soldiers having slowly given up the short curved bladed hanger leaving only officers and senior non commissioned officers with swords.

By the closing years of the 18th Century, the armies of Europe all followed a similar structure with their cavalry divided into Heavy and

Light. The weapon of the Light Cavalry was the sabre, a broad bladed single edged weapon with a curved cutting edge and a simple hilt consisting of pommel, grip and cross guard which gave little hand protection. To afford added hand protection, the cross guard was extended and bent around as a bow and joining the pommel at the top of the sword. This became known as the knuckle bow or (because of the shape) the stirrup hilt. There were, even in the early days of regulation, individualists and they added to this simple guard with extra bars for even greater protection.

The heavy cavalry, larger men on bigger horses, tended to have straight bladed swords with a basket style guard. The basket hilt, familiar today on the Scottish broadsword, was used by the German lands knecht troops in the early 16th century and was the favoured weapon adopted by the mounted troops of Cromwell and the opposing Royalists in the 17th century. By the beginning of the 19th century, it had become the sole preserve of the Scottish sword. The cramped basket style was, later in the century, dispensed with by highland officers on active service and replaced with a simple cross hilt of regimental pattern.

Infantry and later cavalry swords now had in place of the basket hilt, a bowl or knuckle bow made from separate bars or of pierced sheet metal and the best example of these are the 3 bar hilt of the British 1822 Light Cavalry Sword which is still in use today by The Royal Artillery, The Royal Logistics Corps and The Army Air Corps, the 'Gothic' hilt infantry sword of 1822 which was carried up until 1895 by many branches of the British Army and in a different finish is still carried by The Rifles and The Brigade of Guards.

After the Crimean War and the Indian Mutiny during the 1850's, the sword became less important to the Infantry Officer whose primary weapon was the revolver. For the Cavalry, however. It was still a primary weapon and was carried in conjunction with the carbine, revolver and for certain regiments, the lance.

In 1853, after many hundreds of years, the distinction between the swords of the British Light Cavalry and Heavy Cavalry came to an end with the issue of the 1853 Trooper's sword, a cut and thrust weapon. It was of a new design with solid tang and a three bar guard similar to the officer's sword of 1822. In 1864 a similar sword followed with a solid guard pierced with a Maltese Cross pattern which gave further protection. This pattern was again 'tinkered' with in 1882 with disastrous results. Regrettably the quality of the blades was extremely poor and many of these swords which had been made abroad because of cost, failed in the campaign in Egypt in 1882-1884. This failure in military supplies from boots to bayonets and swords to cartridges prompted an enquiry and a War Office Committee to investigate. As a result of deliberations and consultations, the committee failed to produce anything that was novel and the pattern of cavalry sword of 1885 and 1890 are virtually the same in appearance.

However in the opening years of the 20th century some serious thought was given to the cavalry sword in Britain and after trials and deliberations the 1908 sword was produced and although disliked by Edward VII was approved. The officer's version followed in 1912. It has been described by most authorities as the most perfect military sword ever designed, but it came too late to have much effect on the fields of France in 1914-1918.

HOUSEHOLD CAVALRY TROOPER'S SWORD

The only other main change in the 19th century was for Infantry officers and those carrying the infantry sword. In 1892, their gilt Gothic hilt sword was ordered a straight 'dumbbell' blade with only the last few inches sharpened. In 1895, the gilt hilt was replaced by a sheet metal one with piercing, ornamentation and cipher. In 1897 came the final change, more a sartorial tinker than redesign, when the inside of the guard was ordered to be lapped over or turned down to avoid the guard chaffing the uniform!

This sword has, except for change in cipher, been in use ever since and is till made today. The 1912 Cavalry sword is still the current pattern as is the much older pattern 1822 three bar hilted sword.

INFANTRY OFFICER'S SWORD

The Royal Navy sword has undergone small changes since 1827, mainly in blade shape which was regularised in 1846 and finally in 1929, while the sword of the Royal Air Force has remained the same, except for cipher change, since its official adoption in 1925.

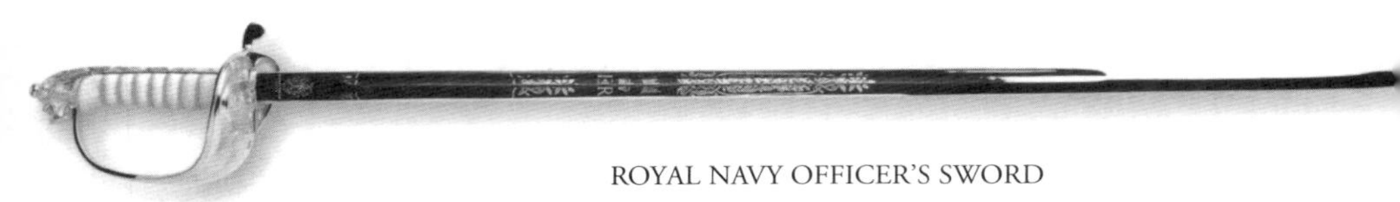

ROYAL NAVY OFFICER'S SWORD

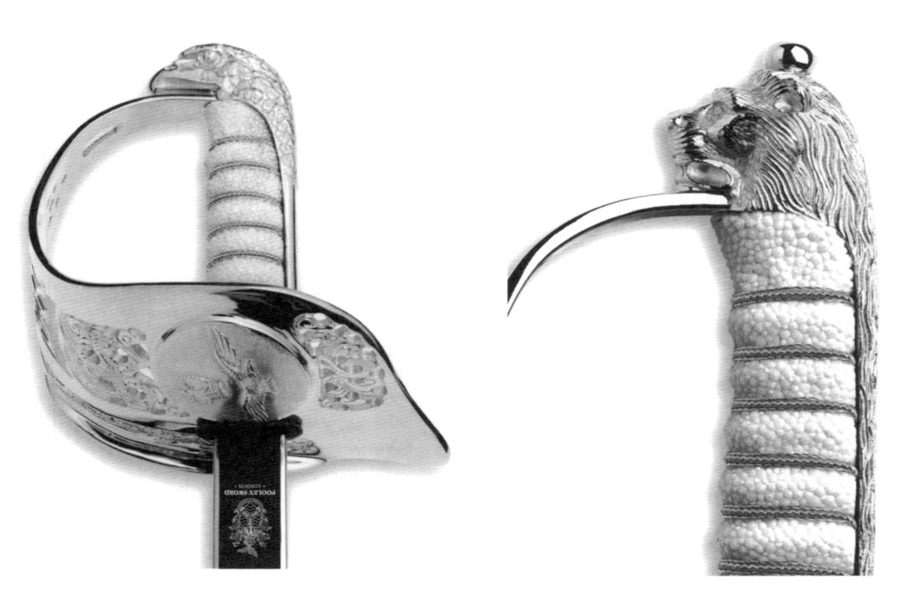

ROYAL AIR FORCE OFFICER'S SWORD HILT

ROYAL NAVY OFFICER'S SWORD HILT

ROYAL AIR FORCE OFFICER'S SWORD

Swordsmiths in England

Although the blacksmith has been a craftsman in England since the earliest days, it was only in the reign of James I (1603-1625) that an infusion of foreign skill made it possible for England to produce sword blades which compared in quality with those of the mid-European states.

1n 1620 there opened on Hounslow Heath a smithy for the manufacturing of sword blades which employed a large percentage of European swordsmiths. Hounslow Heath at that time stretched for five miles along the road west of Hounslow (which had been known in the Domesday Book as 'Honeslaw'). This was only a village, and the Heath purely an open space on which the villagers grazed their cattle. In later years the Heath became famous for highway robbery and gibbets were to be seen on both sides of the road. The sword-smithy was in existence when Charles I came there with his troops in 1642.

The swordsmiths of Hounslow, whose names are still on record today, were—Joseph Jenekes, who came from Solingen, Johann Kindt, also from Solingen, and Benjamin Stone, who was one of the English swordsmiths who joined them there.

The factory was well established and organised at the time of the civil war, and supplied the parliamentary party with a large number of swords. With the growth of the factory more and more immigrants came across; names that are known being—Johan Hopple, Peter Munsten, and Recordus Hopkins.

In the 1660s they apparently lost interest in the Hounslow factory and all of them except Kindt, returned home. Kindt, however, changed his name to Kennett, became a naturalised Englishman, and stayed on.

Naturally, this was but one factory which supplied sword blades, but there is no doubt that at the time it was probably the most successful.

In 1690 Herman Mohll started the Hollow Sword Blade Company at Shotley Bridge near Newcastle.

This company prospered until 1703, when Mohll got into trouble with the law through smuggling sword blades into the

SPANISH RAPIER
16TH-17TH CENTURY

country from Germany, and very soon the Hollow Blade Company went into liquidation. However, it re-opened immediately under the name of Herman Mohll & Son and continued to run for the next 21 years under that name.

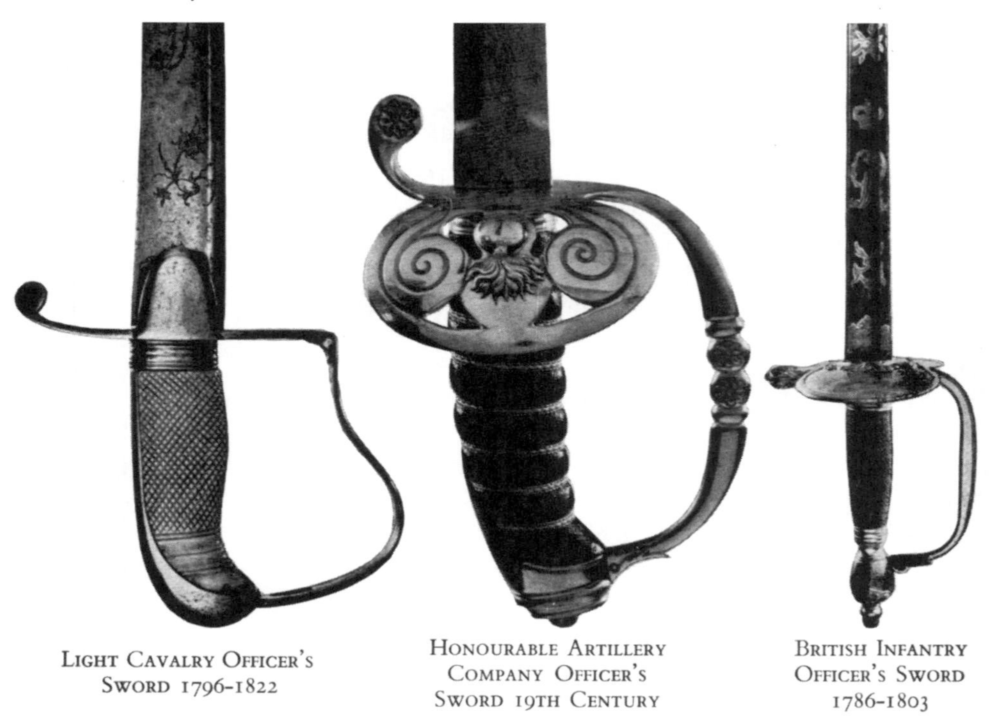

Light Cavalry Officer's Sword 1796-1822

Honourable Artillery Company Officer's Sword 19th Century

British Infantry Officer's Sword 1786-1803

The development of the Sword over thousands of years has given us many varieties of Blade and Hilt. Blades-with cutting edges on both sides, single edged Blades, Straight Blades, Curved Blades and Blades purely for thrusting. Hilts have varied from simple grip and cross-guard, natural in use but giving very little protection, to complicated basket-hilts, giving ample protection against the cut but none against the thrust and cramping the hand so as to make swordplay most difficult. It was not until 1908 when a British War Office Committee, which had sat intermittently since 1884, produced the 1908 pattern British Cavalry Troopers' Sword, which is reputed to be the most perfect Sword ever designed. A great triumph, but unfortunately it came at a time when the Sword, as a weapon of war, was completely outmoded.

Sword making in the late 18th century and early 19th century concentrated around Birmingham where not only were the needs of the army and navy satisfied but blades were made for the finer officer's swords for the London makers. London 'makers' were mainly jewellers, hatters and outfitters and were more sword assemblers from parts bought in, suitably embellished and ornamented under their direction according to the whim of the purchaser. That is not to say a free hand was allowed as there were, by the 1800's, regulations to govern the style of the weapon.

These, as we know, were more often than not flouted, which is explained by the great number of 'variations on a theme' that exist today in museums, collections and available for collectors from auction houses and specialist dealers.

The names of the manufacturers of the Birmingham Houses at this time were a mixed bunch, some superb craftsmen and others good makers capable of turning out government work at the right price. Names such as Harvey, Osborne, Reeves, Mole and others supplied the majority of swords required by the Government.

REEVES'S FACTORY 1854

They also supplied London 'makers' with blades and sometimes complete swords. As the 19th century wore on, many of these Houses fell by the wayside so that by 1869, the only manufacturer left able to completing Government work was Robert Mole and Sons, who had first started making sword in 1835.

Perhaps the most famous name in swords, Wilkinson, did not start making swords until 1844 and then for officers only. Wilkinsons unique 'Proof' of his blades by his 'sword epprovette' (essentially a blade bending machine) meant that unlike previously with poor methods of testing, his blades were subjected to the most rigorous bending and striking before being placed in the hands of the purchaser.

SWORD BLADE BEND TEST

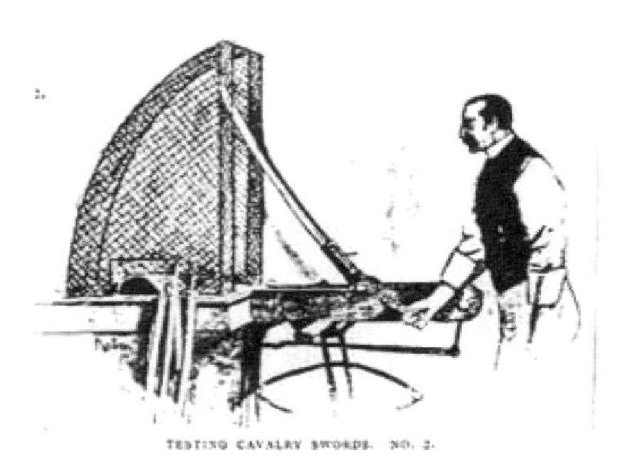

SWORD BLADE STRIKE TEST

As the years progressed, they started supplying their swords to tailors and outfitters as well as from their headquarters at 27 Pall Mall. In 1887, having bought Reeves of Birmingham in 1883, Wilkinsons entered the Government contract market competing with Mole for orders. At this time of change and a more scientific approach to sword design, Wilkinson and Mole supplied their expertise to War Office Committees considering new edged weapons and influenced the design but more importantly the improvement in testing of blades and swords.

During the First World War, both Wilkinson and Mole produced huge quantities of cavalry swords and bayonets and still managed to keep supplying the private purchases of officers, who were still required to carry them. In 1920, Wilkinsons absorbed Robert Mole and in 1922 took over the last two small private sword makers, Thurkle and Pillin.

In August 2005, the very distinguished sword makers Wilkinson Sword, who had been established for over two hundred years, ceased trading as sword cutters to concentrate on the more lucrative business of making razor blades.

Robert Pooley, who had been commissioning swords from Wilkinsons for over forty years, purchased from Wilkinsons their drawings, product records, spares and much of their tooling including both heavy and light machinery. A Ryder Mechanical Hammer which was built in 1886, was also amongst the machinery purchased.

Pooley Sword was formed in November 2005 to produce British Military and Commonwealth swords in the 'Wilkinson' tradition of quality and craftmanship, employing ex-Wilkinson craftsmen and technical expertise. All Pooley blades are forged from carbon steel and tested to the highest standards in the traditional way in Sheffield as laid down by Henry Wilkinson. The finished sword is finally etched and finished to the same fine standards expected by the British and Commonwealth Armed Forces.

Pooley Sword is established as the leading supplier of swords to the British Armed Forces and MOD as well as many Commonwealth and Overseas Defence Forces.

Manufacture

Swords are still produced using traditional methods of manufacture. Blades are made from a single billet of high-carbon steel, before being hand ground to the final shape, hardened and tempered, then hand polished to a mirror finish. Finally, they are acid etched with the required pattern or as specified by the customer.

The hilt or guard is cast in brass or pressed in steel before being-shaped, mirror polished and gold or nickel electro-plated, according to customer requirements. The grip core is carved from wood or HIP, then covered in fish-skin before being bound with gold or silver-plated wire. Each sword is assembled by a skilled craftsman.

Scabbards are made to the same exacting standards as the swords. The scabbard bodies are produced either from rawhide leather or wood covered with pig or goat-skin. A team of inspectors ensures that the quality of the sword is maintained to the fine standards expected by the British armed forces.

Pooley Sword can supply all British Military and Commonwealth Swords.

Pooley Sword also undertake refurbishment of swords to the highest standards. Each refurbishment is different and the sword will be individually assessed before the commencement of the work.

BASKET HILTED BROADSWORD

Sword Publications

Observations on Swords 1844 & 1894	*Henry Wilkinson*
Observations on Swords 18th Edition	*Henry Wilkinson*
The Evolution of Swords	*John Wilkinson-Latham*
British Military Sword	*John Wilkinson-Latham*
British Cut & Thrust Weapons	*John Wilkinson-Latham*
Mr Wilkinson of Pall Mall, Volume 1	*Robert Wilkinson-Latham*
Mr Wilkinson of Pall Mall, Volume 2	*Robert Wilkinson-Latham*
The Swords & Records of Robert Mole	*Robert Wilkinson-Latham*
The History of the F S Knife	*Robert Wilkinson-Latham*
Wilkinson Sword Patterns & Blade Rubs	*Robert Wilkinson-Latham*
Pictorial History of Swords & Bayonets	*Robert Wilkinson-Latham*

Know your Sword

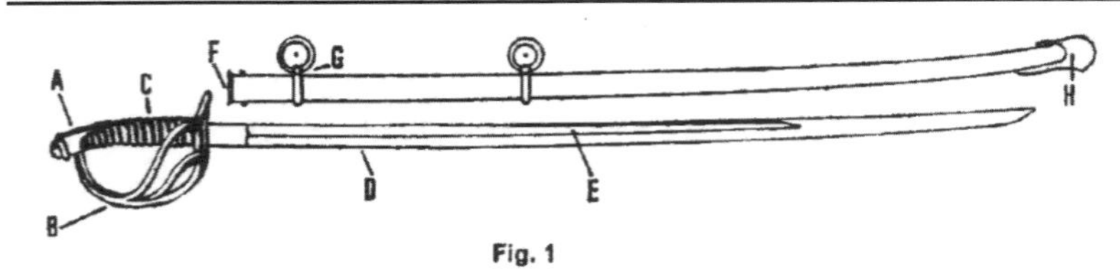

Fig. 1

Sword Parts – Fig 1

A - Cap pommel; **B** - Guard; **C** - Grip; **D** - Cutting edge; **E** - Fuller or Groove; **F** - Scabbard Mouthpiece; **G** - Band & ring for suspension; **H** - Shoe

Sword Parts – Fig 2

A Tang;

B Shoulder of blade;

C Cutting edge;

D Back of blade;

E Fuller or Groove;

F Pommel;

G Knuckle guard with quillons;

H Grip;

I Ferrule;

J Shell guard;

K Guard;

L Slot for sword knot;

M Top nut;

N Pommel & backpiece;

O Under nut;

P Grip;

Q Ferrule.

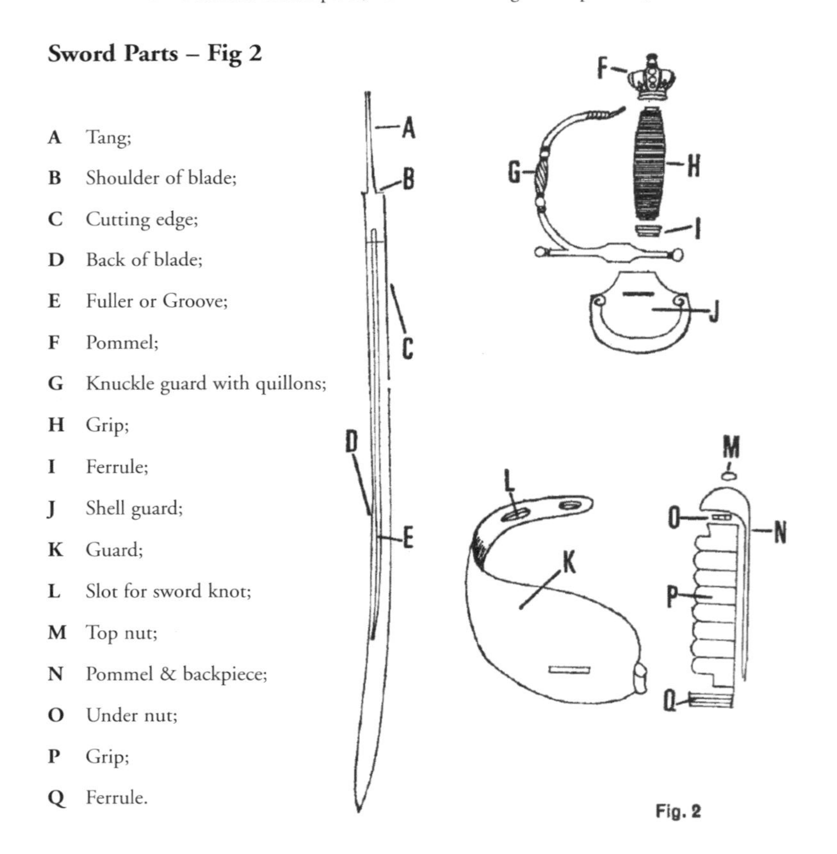

Fig. 2

Sword Facts

Centre of Gravity and Centre of Percussion

This is NOT the balance of the sword, which when held is the feel of the weapon that results from the relative position of the centre of gravity and the centre of percussion.

In lighter swords, these two points are further apart than in heavier swords. They are closer together in a straight blade than in a curved blade and so nearer in a thrusting blade than in a cutting blade. The centre of Percussion is usually at the broadest part of the blade.

Function of the blade 'Groove' or Fuller

One of the most important requirements of a military sword is that the blade is stiff. There is no advantage in a blade for cutting, thrusting or guarding where there is too much flexibility. It is often assumed that the flexibility of the blade denotes a good blade, even better if the point can be sprung to touch the guard! Not so, this error arises from confusing flexibility with elasticity of the steel, which is necessary for a good blade.

By forging the fuller or groove in a blade, the blade is made lighter, but also stiffer and more difficult to bend, because we are in essence bending an arch in on its crown and the more we push to bend the blade, the more resistance there is.

Pooley Sword Guarantee

That this sword blade is forged from special sword steel under our direction and is warranted to have passed the high tests of PROOF demanded by the MOD (British Ministry of Defence). In the event of any damage being done to the blade of this sword, or the sword being allowed to get rusty, it is requested that the weapon is returned to us at once for our inspection.

– Made in England –

Certificate of Proof

No: ....

Type: ....

Proofed: ....

– **POOLEY SWORD LTD** –

1 Highdown House | Shoreham Airport

West Sussex | BN43 5PB | Tel: 01273 467277

Email: **enquiries@pooleysword.com**

LONDON - SHEFFIELD - SHOREHAM

www.pooleysword.com